Calamity's Compass:
Poems for Finding One's Way

Kirstin Eventyr

Dedication:
To Malidoma Some

Acknowledgments

My heart leaps with gratitude to the editors of the following publications that published some of these poems: Blue Heron Review, Gnashing Teeth Publishing: Making Room Zine, Halfway Down the Stairs and the Trillium Awakening Newsletter.

This collection is inspired by my time with Malidoma Some and his brilliantly embodied cosmology and community ritual approach to life. Receiving his indigenous wisdom changed my life and I will never be the same. Alongside Malidoma; Francis Weller opened my awareness to the power of sacred poetry. His own depths and teaching gifts remain with me. Many of these poems began with Joanne Lee's Create! Write process. It has been an invaluable tool, along with the gift of her guidance. Subhaga Crystal Bacon remains a huge inspiration and is largely responsible for this collection coming into existence. Her Poetry of Awakening class, her countless edits of my work and her indefatigable passion for poetry are a blessing beyond description. My fellow writers: Kendra Kehde, Micke Mastro, Heather Reed for your appreciations and wonderings. Thanks to Eileen Keller, Alice Sharrett and Margit Bantowsky for your support and encouragement, I would not have had the courage to put this little book out there if it wasn't for you. Additionally, Queen Mae Butters and Anne Bauer have encouraged me and provided structure for me to keep writing. Finally, my beloved Jens Eventyr, whose constancy, love and support make everything I do better.

Acknowledgments	3
The Geography of No Map	8
Exact Coordinates	9
Thank Goodness	10
Step beyond what is visible	11
Another name for God	13
How You Belong	14
The Pain Initiation	16
How to live through the impossible	17
The Body	19
Earth is my origin story	20
Consummate Your Life	21
The Storm We Need	22
The Great Marriage	23
Wear My Body and Call it Home	24
Pleasure	26
I Need A New Story	27
Yes, You.	28
Abecedarian for the End of the World	29
Breaking to Become	30
Love in Leaving	31
How to Be Human: A Pantoum	32

The Golden Light	33
Fail!	34
World As Kin	35
Plan to be Defeated	36
The moment I was born there were bees in the air	37
Inevitability	39
If you want to grow up	40
Weathering	41
Predator	42
Welcome	44
Facing the Unfaceable	45
Underworld's Embrace	47
Muse	48
Renewal	49
If the only word	51
Risk Kinship	52
Another Way	53
Intuition	54
The Roar	55
Abolition	58
The Way You Need It to Be	59
Enough is Our Middle Name	61

Death	62
Symptom	63
Core Paradox 2	64
Get Weirder	65
Ritual	66
Reclaiming my Heart	67
Gravity	68
Life Cycle	69
Let Love Satisfy	70
Loss	72
Ask the Water	73
Hyper-masculine	74
Hyper-Feminine?	75
Falling into Freedom	76
Limitation as Liberation	78
Oracle	79
About the author	80

The Geography of No Map

Calamity is the name of the school you attend;
Chaos, the headmistress.

The experts have all been banned,
you, hurled from the empty bed,
ache to find the one right way.

Walk the geography of no map,
as you try to throw off the shreds of inflicted
knowledge that barricade the Mystery.

Your genius hides inside of helplessness.
Yes, there, great wonder.
Inside is the only direction.

Notice how the structures that
are not your own, entwine you.

Untangle these threads:
ancestral, cultural, familial.

Send them home and see
the weave of your own cloth.
It will take you where you need to go.

Exact Coordinates

When you are made to feel your body
is a curse upon you, it poisons
the only oracle you have.

Draw from a different type of currency.
You've spent everything you have
pretending to be okay.

Now shame inhabits
where soul has been banished.

Look to the body,
worn and wounded,
it carries the coordinates
of the exact location
to invite soul back in.

Thank Goodness

Praise to Failure!
Praise to Defeat!

~the only ones
who have the courage

to break us
from the currents
of conditioning.

Normalcy is a poison,
that setback pulls,
straight from our cells.

True defeat has no repair,
thank goodness,
it will have its way with us.

Step beyond what is visible

In the world beyond what is visible
there is no you.

This is why the flowers are always winking at you,
why the wind plays with your hair,
and the water so carefully fits herself around you . . .

this is their only chance at you.

You are eternity packed into your person.

If you part the leaves and step beyond
what is visible you unbecome you.

To be

here

is to become

One—
        heartfelt,
        aching,
        liquid,
        sweet,
        light-filled,
        lost—
what are all the adjectives?
Throw them in.

This is you.
Not one thing left out.

You are the One Everything.

Another name for God

Gravity,
ever steadfast,
you hold
each one
so close
and never let go.

Generous equalizer,
pull me
into communion,
that I may find
the trust
to open.

How You Belong

    1.

You are made of bone, by God!
Bone and Light and dripping peaches.

There is a shaman in there too.

Always lighting fires,
offering libations,
plying you with prayer.

She's the one who chose your husband for you,
her and your buckling knees.

In the dream: his image,
the snow goose aloft with his mate,
captured in a silver frame
hung from your family tree.

No denying he's home to you.
Home comes in any form you call love.

You have a home inside the gladiola, inside the parrot tulip,
in the way the breeze moves familiar around you,
in the folks that welcome you as you are.

It's a good thing life is as generous with beauty as it is with loss.
How else could we ever go on?

2.

Place your hand on your heart and know you are home.

This is the only you you will ever be.

Take this moment in your hands
hold it like you would a body of water,
plunge in.

Find your way to the bottom,
to the soft earthen place below.

Let yourself be known by the spirits there.
They have something to teach you
about the preciousness of bones
and the Light that makes its home
in their hollow.

This is how you belong:
Know the Light
Welcome the Bones
Find your Home in each other.

The Pain Initiation

When you dive
deep enough
into that pool,

beyond
the feeling of
assault and
invasion,

there lives
in those depths
meaning and purpose

calling you back
from the remoteness
of spirit.

How to live through the impossible

First face the darkness.
 Do not turn away.
 You must know
 what it is you are braving.

Next taste every loss,
 let each one break you.
 Forget all the old ways,
 you have entered the chrysalis.

Now re-find the wild in you:
 go barefoot,
 growl until your eyes shine,
 make a poisonous plant your ally,
 bite something with all your strength,
 break your dishes.

Listen for the ones who have known you
since before you were born.
 Ask them what is sacred.
 Promise yourself to whatever they say.
 Worship it.
 Stay close to the bone.

One day, wings warm and heart
clear of the tangle of pain,
you will light upon the life
you are already living.

Now you have no shield,
only an unbending
loyalty to yourself and
it can take you
anywhere.

The Body

Oracle of all, clever diviner
        of flesh, tears, sinew and salt,
out of each taste of pain
        you open us to the great way.

We greet you—
most devoted of all—
our path remains your medium.

Flawless guide, it is you who brings
light into the depths, you who seeds
our dreams with direction, you who ignites
our longing for the evolutionary step.

By your grace, wielder of access,
we gain entry to the miracle of matter.

Earth is my origin story

Mushroom spores
tip the water wheel,
seeding the clouds,
the sky to open.

We have gotten it all wrong:
the only access to the infinite
is the finite.

Surrender to root and rhizome,
moss, elderberry, honeycomb,
antler and elf.

The reverent earth,
sustenance of soil.

Consummate Your Life

Marry your life right away.
The proposal was accepted long ago,

what are you waiting for?

Let yourself be carried over the threshold
of the house whose name is

Take My Hand.

Now that you are betrothed,
everything has taken this name:

the blooming cherry
the fire-breathing sunset
the lost dog

even you.

The Storm We Need

If the storm,
coming assuredly toward us,
carried on its winds
our secret fulfillment,
we would not see it for the rain.

Where we see destruction,
Chaos sees all,
sees herself as all,
and holds us to her.

Her only prayer ~ our wholeness.

The Great Marriage

Pain is the vehicle
we're always trying to escape,
her destination the holy land.

Trouble speaks the language
you've forgotten,
it's pronounced *radical change*.

Loss opens doorways
obscured by a normal point of view.
Normal is a state of possession we know as dullness.

Illness reveals the cult of infinite velocity,
the compartmentalized, linear fiction
that shuts aliveness down.

Soul seeks the vibrant, the fertile.
Let the rock and rose and wind lead you,
mammal and moon reshape you.

Step out of time into the eternal.
You are the greatness of your spirit.
You are the gateway to your own singularity.

Elope with your greatness;
align with your greatness.
Make aliveness your normal
and see how you thrive.

Wear My Body and Call it Home
      after Maggie Smith

Do you remember when you lived here,
down in the bones?

You are being called back.
Right this minute.

Enter through stillness,
      through welcome,
      through song,
      through your belly
pressed to the Earth.

You know the way.
Every dark corner has a gift for you.
Welcome it.

Each desire,
      to come closer,
      to move away,
takes you farther in.

Every feeling,
      bogged down belly,
      rot in the heart,
      the dooming pulse of fear,
seeks only your hand to hold.

Welcome it.

Every moment you wish it were different,
invites you to the table of belonging.

There is no safer place than here.

Do you hear the body calling you?
With each ache, she says come home.

She has been calling to you for years:
      your yearning, your emptiness,
      your love of the scarlet flower,
      your loneliness, your heart leaping in your chest,
each of these is her voice.

      Come home.
      Come home!
      Come home!!

      I cannot Be without you.

Pleasure

You hold
a faith
that sees
no boundary.

Yours is
the master key,
every lock
your mistress.

I Need A New Story

Ancestors, I have needed you.

Tell me a true story.
Tell me when
everything was beyond repair.
Tell me how there was a path
that rose to meet you. Tell me how
you were never alone.

Please don't tell me the story
of the hero, who with luck
and timing, smarts and a few good friends,
vanquishes the enemy.
There can be no enemies now.

Tell me the story of the upwelling,
how it opens every one of us,
how it connects each one to the other,
how it secures us irrevocably to an
unshakeable source.

Ancestors, we need you now.
Help us to repair what you have left undone.
Tell us the story of how life really loves us,
and it all really matters
and how we can arrive together.

Yes, You.

Unqualified.
Helpless.
Overwhelmed.

Yes, you,
our natural champion.

Competence is a door-closing curse.

Embrace the grace in not knowing.
Welcome your bewilderment
and let yourself be aimed
beyond your grasp.

Abecedarian for the End of the World

Astounded
By the absurd miracle of it all,
Chaos presides over this revolution.
Devoted to the whole bloody mess,
Exalted and weeping all the way.
Friend to Evolution,
Granting safe passage to none,
Holding hands as we go
Into the unknown.
Joined by every last one:
Kingdom, phylum, class, order, all family.
Lashing ourselves to the
Mast pole, each wave calls us by
Name. Into the drink, into the dark
Out of our depth
Pulled by our prayers, down into the
Quiet.
Receptive at last, the
Shape of our
Transformation
Unfolds in the swell of the eternal. Blessed
Vessel, the path itself. The
Whorl of galaxies reflecting a
Xenial co-creation. It's
You, madam Chaos, hidden
Zygote in the flesh ushering our way Home.

Breaking to Become

As a cicada blooms
out of its skin,

I, too, feel
the ache
of exoskeleton

and what longs
to live
in full expression:

to make a friend
of breaking
to become

the body
in surrender to
what will remain

once it shrugs off
its architecture
of protection.

Love in Leaving

Sometimes you choose your losses.
You say when and why and how.

>But can you leave and continue
>to Love? Can you not throw anyone

from your heart as you go?
When you see all the blessedness

>and know it is not for you,
>when you feel the turmoil of distrust

and bow to it as your teacher,
when you feel the needs of others call

>to you, and trust you are not their keeper,
>this is the time of your salvation.

This is the time to trust things as they are,
to let the tower topple.

>To listen to the truth of disappointment
>and leave with a stinging heart of gratitude

even as the tears stream.

How to Be Human: A Pantoum

Live like you are a candle burning,
your flame licking out the bowl.
Or live silk-shaped and open, your lips a full moon.
Live your likeness to this miracle, this being human.

Your flame licking out the bowl,
everyday a new feast, the body's devotion.
Live your likeness to this miracle, this being human.
Drink deep the seeds settling sweet in your lap.

Everyday a new feast, the body's devotion
brings you to your knees, weeping for your luck - this day!
Drink deep the seeds settling sweet in your lap.
They grow through slow hips carrying light from the black soil.

Brought to your knees, weeping for your luck - this day,
you are the dark earth, the sprout, the blossom and the fruit,
growing out through slow hips, carrying light from the black soil.
Now savor how the possible finds home in your bones.

You are the dark earth, the sprout, the blossom and the fruit.
Live like you are the candle burning,
savor how the possible finds home in your bones
and live silk shaped and open, your lips the full moon.

The Golden Light

Instinct rises
from your deepest moorings -
like a dark spring
you never knew.

You reveal the gesture
wounds make
when left unaccompanied:
        the way they cannot keep time and never age,
        the way their shell grows rough and sharp,
        how nothing gets in.

To us you are a golden light that never sleeps
Go into that dark with your golden self,
let us hold you as you go.

        Know all you encounter has come to heal.
        Know the worst has already happened.
        Know your love is the true healer.

Fail!

The bigness
of what you pursue
requires it.

Demand
impossibility.

World As Kin
        after Sophie Strand

I am transspecies:
a coalescing cluster of chaos,
a swarm of pollenating possibility.

I am foliage, vining and twining,
ferment and fruit. Can you feel
your heart, too, entangled with the grove?

The stream tells us stories
of mineral and melt.
This language is still alive inside you.

Listen to remember,
revive the dream,
the living somatic mystery.

Be the Goddess where every cell
belongs
to every other being.

Become the horned God:
human, animal, home.
Dilate.

You are everything you perceive.

Plan to be Defeated

Discomfort is a wind;
it propels you into the reunion
your soul calls for.

Plan to be defeated.
Catch the dream and ask:

What can be restored?

No longer
cultivate the lie
of pretense.

Be explicit.
Pursue pain.
Welcome conflict.

Make offerings
to constriction.

This altar points to
a breach in intimacy.

Find the rupture,
settle into the tear
it will teach you
the way home.

The moment I was born there were bees in the air

their familiar buzz welcoming me home again.
They alighted on my mother's hair and shoulders,
they crawled under the cuffs of my father's shirt.
They danced the dance that bees do to alert
each other of the location of a
blossom—now they will always find me.

Winters after winter my child's
heart wanders, begging bowl outstretched.
My mother gone 50 years,
this nectar eludes me still,
a bee flits from paper
flower to paper bloom.
No substitute lasts.

The Queen takes me
under her wings
pulsing her
pattern of
belonging
into my
emptiness.

No substitute
but colony,
they cover me like
water: ear lobes and
toes, the corners of my
eyes and crook of my knee.

Everything becomes this hum.

The bees whispering "surrender."
Hovering in my hollows their
wings sing "trust." Vibrating each atom
into sweet resonance. My bowl fills with
honey, still, the hunger swarms my heart. I make
myself like larva, begin again and open.

Inevitability

The wound
has its own purpose.

Not linear,
not rational,

not punishment,
nor failure or flaw,

but mystery
being revealed.

Inevitability is her name.

If you want to grow up

wake up from the trance of
childhood.

Step into the full parental rights
your mother and father lost
now that you are grown.

Your child inside
      takes the truth from your mouth
      sacrifices your heart for approval
      self-betrayal is her daily bread.

Gather her into arms that wholly welcome.
Her heart pressed to yours,

the only one who knows
her from the inside out.

She will fight
      cling
      demand
to remain faithful to those who hurt her.

Her empty hope
      extinguished
      only through
the deep embrace of
your heart.

Weathering

The storm that swept you in is named True Blue;
its winds are equal to the gifts you carry.

>Your gifts are called into action,
>as the other world holds your hand.
>
>To fight the storm is to join it.
>To flee the storm is to be pursued.
>To stand still is to be swept away.
>
>Walk with dignity into the storm;
> it belongs to you.

Predator

The one who comes from inside
       trashes your tenderness,
       tears down your dreams,
       brutalizes each and every flaw.

Her sacred purpose:
your survival.

She sits down
only
when you step up.

Be your own source
or be her prisoner.

She is the industrial
world's monster.

She invented
       cages,
       tranquilizers,
       police.

She seeks to colonize
the whole universe
starting with you.

Be an abolitionist.
Begin from the inside out.

Become a liquid rebel.
Licking the face
with bared teeth

encompassing
the one
who makes
you small.

Welcome

The galaxies pour their light
into your open hand,
reminiscing about your kinship.

You don't have to earn
that kind of generosity.

It lays the welcome mat
at your feet and just like that,
there is nowhere else to go.

The welcome adheres
to the soles of your feet
and your money is no good here.

Your belonging is secured
as the bloom of galaxies
calls you kin.

Facing the Unfaceable

Chaos comes rattling.

She sees the time has come,
she sees there is no other way,
she sees there is finally room.

She must find the place
where wound meets defense
and slip right between, so the harm
you have wrought can be seen.

This harm has come to save you.
It has come to lighten the load,
it has come for redemption,
it has come so you can make amends.

We don't end the game with clean hands.

All along, the bramble of our original wound
wraps round us, drags behind us, envelopes us;
leaving behind berries and regretful seeds.
Slicing those, our closet kin.

There is no other way.

Eat every berry.
Make a tincture of the thorns,
take it morning, noon and night.
Peel each briar into strips, dry in the sun.

Once they have taken on the color of your true name
weave the fibers into a basket shaped like you.

Do this every year
for the rest of your life and
then come Home.

Underworld's Embrace

Needs, the heaviest stones,
drop down beyond knowing.

You are the queen of this wasteland
waking to the well of sadness below.

You climb the rungs of rib and bone.
Falling to the bottom over again

through blizzards and snakes,
black wounds and owl feathers.

Truth is the bare ground
that takes you into her lap.

What happened to you wasn't about you,
sometimes the waves devastate the shore.

Muse

Call her
    Chaos,
    Great Mother,
    Mystery,
    God.

She won't take your name.

She embeds herself in blood and breath.
Matter has seized her.

She is the reverse of a snake shedding it's skin.
More and more she packs herself in.

Spacious union
consumed by human form:

    you are stone,
    you are light.

Renewal
> after: Many Breasted Goddess Meets Snake
Goddess painting by Reda Rackley

When you, with 100 breasts,

pour milk and honey all day long,
and have been finally used up,

when you dream of having your own dreams,

this is the time to call to the snake sister inside:
> slither-and-bright,
> undulation and tongues,
> hissing and fangs,
who loves you like no one else can.

She wraps round you reminding you of your edges,
she shows how to hold on to what belongs to you,
how you must save something for yourself.

You, many breasted Mother, open your fists,
there is an eye in the middle of each palm.
They see every gift given and every gift received.

Place your palms over your heart and see
what it has to teach you about your giving.

You can spend a lifetime feeding the world.
Imagine what can be fed if you start with yourself?

Let the snakes lick you with their feathery tongues.
Let them lap up the sweat and tears,
and leave you shimmering in the night.

The snakes shimmy up your spine
and show you the pathway to the Goddess
lies not in what you offer but in what
you are.

If the only word

        you ever spoke

               was

                      no

I would

                    still

             Love you.

Risk Kinship

Open as a wing,
nothing to defend.

Let life imprint upon you
the signature:
> of nettle,
> pine cone,
> beaver
> and stillness.

You, heartwood of you,
> risk the merge.

Take in the one-time
concoction of you
commingled with
> snow melt,
> the morning's amber light,
> the crescent moon shine.

This moment in time
we have never needed each other more.

Bind yourself to Life to break the spell of emptiness
that has fallen over our Earth home.

Another Way

Oh, great beast of complexity,

      set me free!

Take me to the ocean.

      Show me how the waves
           find each other again

as they are pulled out to sea.

Intuition

You weren't made for knowing.
You are a sealed mystery even to yourself.
You are the great unknown.
You are the living magic of Being the answers.

Follow it back to its deep source
where the unknown waits
to make your acquaintance.

Inside you it sings day and night
hoping your ears will catch
the thread and not let go.

Listen for the clear bell tone
of truth that only you can hear.

The Roar

The bears had all been skinned,
and hung from the trees.
It is night, and those
      her trademark knots,
        her bloody ink on the knife.

In the sterilized light
of morning, the trees are bare—
      she is nowhere.
      I must be making this all up.

I argue her goodness—
She is the Light itself—
as my elders point
      to the blood running a dark shadow
      from beneath her white robes.

Fur dull, teeth filed,
my muzzle sinks to my chest.
What is wrong with me?
How could this be? This is not me!

An upwelling,
a fire kindled,
my blood runs hot once again,

    the   ROAR   finally   comes, pouring:

      half-digested snakes
frightened birds,

     frozen fire,

                  unspoken spiders,

jailed down justice,

          the spittle of so many lines in the sand.

Breath comes full now.

     eyes clear,

     muzzle lifted,

                a rebellion restored.

When someone tries to tame you
roar right away.

     Feel the growl of protection vibrate through your
bones.
     See the mountain lion leap from your lips
     Hear the hiss of *thisss stopsss here!*

You are the wild
through and through.

Nothing needs to change
about you.

Abolition

Live a life

of good behavior

                and look back

                                              from

eternity

                        saying

                        you did

                        good

prison work.

The Way You Need It to Be

The enchantment
you speak:

    It shouldn't be this way,

is a curiosity-killing curse,
cutting off your source
like slicing a root.

    It shouldn't be this way.

You speak this
incantation
in a voice
that believes
it has a right to only ease.

    It shouldn't be this way.

Ease alone
would waste you,
my friend.

Life owes you
the opportunity
to wrestle your way into
becoming yourself.

The way it is

is the way you
need it to be.

Enough is Our Middle Name

With each wave of lack,
each feeling of flaw,
and each question of worth,
we bid to earn the title of enough.

Enough is our middle name
placed there to remind us
who we really are.

See how the small sips satiate?
See how alive we are and complete?
There is nothing to chase.

Death

    is

        no

            one's

                enemy.

Symptom

Drought dries up the buoyant spirit; ice caps melt
resolve, the heart sinks down following each extinction.

You are an ecosystem of Life force,
an elaboration of our ancestors,

a conglomerate of culture living its
expression through your cells.

Call this pain a ramification.

You are a synthesis of collective history:
the flames of the witch trials rise up the spine,
the holocaust hollows out your chest,
this headache: the press of the patriarchy.

Anxiety is not your home;
it climaxes through this vessel
in revolutionary uproar.

Wholeness is your name,
and innermost every cell,
a devotional mystery

singing a call and response with the
nature of all things.

Core Paradox 2

The body is the portal in.
This dark Source bears your Light,
swallow gravity to begin.

Trust your senses, know your season,
welcome, too, the bones of night.
The body is the portal in.

A pressure suit, this being human,
brings us to the edge of flight.
Swallow gravity to begin.

Listen closely, claim your region,
dwell in root to know the height.
The body is the portal in.

Welcome all the pain as kin,
savor everyday delight.
Swallow gravity to begin.

There is no end, we only deepen.
Here the soul chose to alight.
The body is the portal in,
swallow gravity to begin.

Get Weirder

You know how you are really weird?

Not that you think or believe weird things,
but are a weird thing yourself?

The experiential weirdness
that only you can ever really know?

You just have to keep taking it further.
Go deeper with that.

Trust me.

Ritual

Surrender to the
incomprehensible.

Bring all of you.

The pain of shame,
defectiveness,
conformity,
will debilitate you

until

you bow
to them,
as the only saviors.

Pain lays the path
and derangement
is holy ground.

Your mess,
your wildness
reclaimed,
are your guardians—
they know
the way home.

Reclaiming my Heart
       after Bukowski

There is a predator in my heart who is my warden.
She reveals to me the dark thoughts of others,
reminds me to be small.
I rally against her but she doesn't see.

There is a predator in my heart who stands in for me.
She hates me most of all.
She knows my every inch,
the secret weakness of my needs.

She is a predator who never stops,
though I douse her in wine, and try to keep her still.
Her claws show no mercy.
Her teeth rip into my dreams.
Sometimes she comes right out of my mouth.

The predator in my heart wants to get out.
My friends withstand her influence
and show me how she lies.
She speaks my childhood fears
and hasn't grown at all.

There is a predator in my heart,
I've let her out myself
when all is quiet and we are alone.
I'm showing her how things change,
training her to speak the truth.
She is mine and I am hers.

Gravity

Enter the Earth,
> find home here.

Go deeper still.
> Become matter-full.

Gravity is your ally,
> she'll never let you go.

Trust her embrace.
> You can let go completely.

You can let go completely.
> You can let go completely

into the deep body territory
> of home.

Gravity takes you deeper.
> How full can you be?

Saturated with Self,
> swallow gravity down

into your bones.
> And become home.

Life Cycle

In the dawn of your life
your starseed took root
and look at that light!

At high noon legs flying, arms juggling 1000 things
your mind tracks 10,000 more
as you try to work your way into belonging.

By evening
you learn there is no earning
the Love of Life.

In the deep night
there is only Being
and it is finally enough.

Let Love Satisfy

In our deepest heart
Love satisfies us.

She holds us so close,
rubs her cheek against our hearts,
pours rose petals all over the bed,
cradles our cheeks in her hands saying
You, it is you and only you my dearest.

Each soft feather smooths into place.
The breath, slow and deep,
even the belly lays down her shield.

Love does that, you know?
Love says
Yes, You!
Yes!
You!
And never falters.

Bewildered with longing
our hearts on tip toe,
hand raised as high as it will go . . .
Pick Me! Pick me!

You need not worry,
you were chosen before your Mother's first breath
and before her Mother's too.

Eternity has been waiting for your arrival.

Have you not noticed how the wind crowds around you?
How the birds sing your name?
How the flowers flirt, eager for your glance?

Life is calling out to you,
moment after moment,
all day long.

Blessing you.
Inviting you.
Belonging to you.

When will there be another you?

All of creation has lined itself up for you:

All the music, its yours.
Every tree, yours.
Each color, yours.
The highest places,
the coldest rock,
the newborn bees they belong to you,
as family belongs to each other.

What if you knew you were Loved like that?

This is the truth of things my friend.
This is the truth.
Lay yourself wide
and let Love satisfy.

Loss

You risk your heart
by loving what lives and dies.

The breeze that touches
and then is gone.

Lean in
as you lose
the form you love.

Lift it gratefully to the sky
as you fall to the ground.

Let the Life you will lose
love you through the loss.

This is human magic:
To break and be made whole by breaking.

Ask the Water

You want radical change,
    effortless change,
        the change that changes everything,
        can't-I-just-get-comfortable-change.

In nature when change is radical
we call it a

    catastrophe.

The caterpillar is the ambassador
of organic change.

    And have you met the Autumn?

    Ask the water how long it took her
    to make the canyon.

Look to the elemental elders to find your way.

Hyper-masculine

Incredulous and fat
with claws and teeth
they cling to the teat
Mine, they say.

The Great Mother says
My creation
    what have you become:
        thieves and slave-makers,
        who spit into the fire.

            Where is your flowering wand?

Reverence casts the kind of light
            that causes the seed to sprout.

Then watch as the lilies lay themselves

open before you.

Hyper-Feminine?

Is the ocean too wet?
Too vast?

Does the ocean give too much?

When has there been too much Love in this world?

The feminine has no boundary, needs no boundary.

Holds when it is time to hold,
releases when it is time to release.

Falling into Freedom

A seed
inside each of us

guides each footfall,
takes our hand as we falter,
ensuring our fall.

It shakes our foundations,
and rocks the roof.
The walls weep,

the ceilings cry out
We can't take much more!
But the shaking doesn't stop,

it can't stop
until every bit of falseness
is shaken free.

The survival strategies fall,
one after another,
and the best laid plans
lay the fuck down.

Finally there is nothing
left to do.
The fight has left you
and you are free.

The holy books have slipped off the shelves

and taken flight.
You don't need them.
The only script you can read anymore

is your own fingerprints,
the whorls of galaxies.

You have become the fundament.
You are the answer.
You are the meaning deepest inside.

Limitation as Liberation

Where do you get off writing poems?
Set your pen down and grieve

how you've never been enough
and never will be, not enough

to make the world
right again or to erase the harm.

There are no off-ramps to who you are, darling.
There is only the whole of you,

the never-another you,
the blowing-it-just-like-you,

the landslide of you, the buttercup of you,
the open eye, the closed door,

the raised ceiling, the deep waters,
the dump truck, the remedy.

You are the all of it.
There it is. So be it.

Oracle

Trust your Life, just as it is.
It too seeks your hand to hold.
It too urges you to believe
that what you find inside
is the path itself.

Your felt sense inside is devoted
to you. Steadfast is it's name.
No one loves you more.

About the author

Kirstin Eventyr is a poet from the southernmost part of the Salish Sea in Washington State, where she has enjoyed a 30 year career as a heart-centered therapist. Her love of flowers, the bodies of all beings and the trustworthiness of the pain inform all aspects of her writing. In her free time she walks the wilds with her beloved husband and their 2 English Bulldogs, Cocoa and Beauford.

www.kirstineventyr.com

Printed in the USA
CPSIA information can be obtained
at www.ICGtesting.com
CBHW032136260924
14967CB00043B/828

9 780990 363149